Mel Bay Presents
CHILDREN'S
Fiddling
Method

VOLUME 2

By Carol Ann Wheeler

A recording and a video of the music in this book are now available. The publisher strongly recommends the use of one of these resources along with the text to insure accuracy of interpretation and ease in learning.

Visit us on the Web at http://www.melbay.com — E-mail us at email@melbay.com

Contents

Credits

Many thanks to:

    John Standefer for suggested chords for accompaniment, and for fine guitar backup on the learning recording.

    Steve Lawrence of Steve Lawrence Phone Co. as recording and mixdown engineer.

    Linda Danielson, my twin fiddle partner, for sharing her twin fiddle parts and her tune (My Cousin's Reel).

How to get the Most out of this book
HOW TO LEARN A FIDDLE TUNE

✔ **READ THE PRINT** – The print will help you learn more about how to play the tune.

✔ **LEARN THE TUNE** – Use your music to learn the tune at your own pace. When you can play the tune all the way through without making stops, then you are ready for the next step!

✔ **LISTEN AND PLAY ALONG WITH YOUR LEARNING RECORDING** – You will find the entire tune played slowly and unaccompanied. It is fun to use earphones. Use your own metronome and practice on your own over a period of time to build your speed up until you feel ready for the next step.

✔ **PLAY ALONG WITH YOUR RECORDING** – Now you are ready to play along with guitar on the final arrangement. While some of the tunes may "feel" fast in the beginning, with time and practice you will be able to build up your tempo.

BOWINGS AND ORNAMENTS – I have written bowings and ornaments that I use and like. Often times I may have different ways to bow, and several ways to play ornaments. You do not have to put in every single ornament that I play. Choose those that you like. If you like my sound on the recording, using the bowing I suggest will help you to get closer to that sound. If you wish to change some bowing, that is perfectly fine!

ABOUT THE MUSIC IN THIS BOOK

MUSICAL EXAMPLES – The musical examples are really little exercises to help you with the tunes. They have repeat marks to indicate that you repeat them as much as you need. On your learning recording you will hear them first played slowly and then played a second time more up to speed.

CHORDS – You will find the chords that are used on your learning recording written in the final arrangement.

The initials "**f.f.**" stand for "fat finger technique," a term I coined to refer to the use of one finger on two different strings at the same time. It may be necessary to not have the finger on its tip, but rather on its side; the fleshy part.

A **curved arrow** ⤵ over a note is my notation to "SLIDE" up into that note.

A **curved arrow** ↘ over a note pointing down is my notation to slide **down** from the note.

A **double curved arrow** like ⤴↘ means to slide *up into* a note and then *down out of* the note.

↘⤴ means to play the note, slide *down* out of the note and then back *up into* the note.

Listening to your learning recording over and over will be a terrific learning aid. If you're not familiar with a tune, listening to the tune several times *before* trying to learn it will speed up the learning process. Listening with ear phones before sleep is also excellent.

Use **earphones** during the learning process and during part of your practice period when you are playing along with me. It is also possible with stereo equipment, to turn the fiddle low, leaving just the guitar for you to practice with.

My hope for you is that with time, after you feel comfortable with my arrangements, you will branch out, maybe adding some ideas from other fiddlers and some of your own ideas to create your own arrangements! **Have fun!**

15-year-old Ryan McKasson of Washington - 1995 National Scottish Fiddle Champion.

Tiffany Wheeler, 1982 National Jr. Jr. Fiddle Champion. (11 years old) – Photo by Joyce Hagan

Below: Grant and Tiffany Wheeler, 1974 (9 and 7 years of age) At right: at ages 4 and 6 years old.

In Memory
Misti Aday, b. 1978-d. 1995. Misti, shown here at age 14, loved playing violin and fiddle and was considering becoming a music teacher.

Dedication

This book is dedicated to my children, Grant and Tiffany, who taught me more about life than I ever taught them about fiddling. It is also dedicated to all of the children, as well as you dear reader, who play fiddle, as it is through you all that our wonderful heritage of old-time fiddle will be preserved.

About the Author

Carol Ann Wheeler   John Standefer

Pickin' & Fiddlin'

Carol Ann Wheeler has an extensive background of over 20 years as a violinist, orchestral member, and string teacher for public and private schools. She has always been fascinated by the sound of the fiddle. In 1974 she began to study and learn how to play old-time fiddle. Intrigued by different styles of fiddling, she became a collector and performer of several: old-time, Texas, trick and show fiddling, cross tunes, Canadian, Scottish, and Irish to list some of the styles she enjoys. Since 1974 she has produced five fiddle albums and has been a contest fiddler, judge, and fiddle workshop teacher. She has performed for ten years through Young Audiences of Oregon and Washington, and has traveled and performed in Japan, Canada, and Scotland, as well as the U.S.

Ms. Wheeler taught her own two children (who both became champion fiddlers) how to play fiddle, starting them at very young ages. Her home contains over 200 fiddle-contest trophies, plaques, etc. Through her fiddle workshops, albums, and performances, she has taught and perpetuated fiddle music to thousands. She and her students have won numerous times on the state, regional, and national levels. As announcer Harry Reeves said at the National Fiddle Contest in Weiser, Idaho, "You name it, she's won it!"

Ms. Wheeler is known for being an energetic and enthusiastic performer and for teaching not just notes, but technique and style as well. She is thrilled to be able to teach and perpetuate the art of old-time fiddling to an even larger scope of people through Mel Bay Publications.

Recording

Equally important to the fiddle student is the *listening recording or the video recording,* where all tunes and music examples are played *slowly* and up to tempo by champion fiddler/master teacher Carol Ann Wheeler, so that at completion of this volume the budding fiddler is not simply *playing the notes* of a fiddle tune, but hopefully playing with a *true* "fiddle style." A solid foundation and understanding of *how to play the fiddle* are laid and the student is ready to progress to more difficult tunes not only in this series, but also those offered in the wealth of fiddle-tune collections from Mel Bay Publications.

Introduction

Dear Fiddlers,

Welcome to Volume 2 of CHILDREN'S FIDDLING METHOD! I have some wonderful tunes waiting for you. I love each and every tune in this collection and I am very excited about sharing my arrangements with you!

Since this second volume will build on the techniques explained in Volume 1, it is most important that you understand those techniques or that you already have a good foundation of fiddling skills. Even though Volume 1 starts at an easy skill level, it progresses rapidly, explaining step-by-step many of the fiddle skills that will be used in the second volume.

Don't let the title fool you. CHILDREN'S FIDDLING METHOD - Vol. 2, while created for children, is also equally perfect for adults (who wish a little T.L.C.), violinists, violin, and fiddle teachers alike. What will separate it from other collections and methods is: the tunes will be played slowly, unaccompanied so that you can hear the notes and how the tune goes. Then an arrangement more up to tempo with backup will also be provided. Your final goal is to play along with me using the available recording.

Included in this volume will be optional twin fiddle parts and tips on twin fiddling. These will be great for teachers to use with their students or fiddlers to play with friends.

All tunes will be broken down into parts for easier learning. New fiddling techniques will be explained. Often different versions will be offered for the same tune. This will not only give the student variety, but gradually the concepts, skills, and ideas explained in the variations can be used in other tunes the student knows or will learn in the future. You will be learning HOW to fiddle, not just to play the notes of a fiddle tune. This will broaden you as a performer. In Volume 2 you will explore several keys. The tunes are ones that I have recorded, performed, and taught for years. Some are very old and have never, to my knowledge, been published before. If you enjoy them as much as I, you have some great fun in store for you, and you will be a part of helping to preserve a little piece of our history!

Enjoy!

Most Sincerely,
your fiddle coach,

Carol Ann

Carol Ann

Lesson #1 - Preparation for Our First Tune – Wake Up Susan

If I had to choose one key as the most popular key for fiddle, I would pick the key of A. Sometime just take note of the audience's reaction when they hear the sounds of a fiddler playing an introduction on the A and E strings. It just makes the audience sit up and take notice.

Let's prepare for WAKE UP SUSAN by reviewing the "fat finger" technique. As you recall when you use ONE finger on TWO strings at the same time, it may be necessary to have it on its side, making it "fatter." We use this f.f. technique in Part 2.

Practice this exercise:

Ex. #1

Now add a high 3 on the G string.
Next time try sliding into this high 3.

Ex. #2

LEARNING TIP:

Did you notice that you are playing first on the bottom *pair* of strings, then the middle *pair* of strings?

It's actually your bowing arm that is doing the work here, and not so much your fingers.

REMINDER: The curved arrows (⌣↗) indicate notes that I like to slide into. To make a slide, you place your finger about a half inch *below* the note and slide up *to* the note. Be careful not to slide past the note.

Now let's learn one possible arrangement of this old-time hoedown.

Lesson #2: Wake Up Susan
Arrangement #1

Wake Up Susan

Traditional
Arrangement by
Carol Ann Wheeler

Key of A
Intro = 2 chops & 4 potatoes

Lesson #3: Variations for Wake Up Susan

Take as long as you wish to learn WAKE UP SUSAN. It would be good for you to feel pretty comfortable with it before starting to learn the variations. We can now use WAKE UP SUSAN to learn about "fiddling" a tune. You may find that many of the techniques you learn here will also work for you in other fiddle tunes.

Let's look at part one first:

Ex. #1

Instead of the two pickup notes: as in Ex. #1, we could use a little scale. I have nicknamed it a "roll-up."

Ex. #2

Many times in fiddling, I will take one LONG note and make it into TWO shorter notes. I call this "doubling." It makes the music seem a little more busy. Here in measure 1 is a perfect example of where you can use doubling.

Ex. #3

Measure 1 the original way:

Part 1

Ex. #4

Now measure 1 with "doubling":

Ex. #5

Or you could use the "roll-up" and "doubling" like this:

In the first half of measure 3, we could add an E note on the D string ("fat finger one") to give some nice harmony.

Ex. #6

Then in the second half of measure 3 is a nice place to add a "flick" (a grace note). As you practice this little lick go for a feeling of relaxation in your left hand. You should practice this lick until it is easy for you.

Ex. #7

In measure 8 (the last measure of Part 1) it sounds good, I think, when you sometimes let the open E string "drone" as you come down the notes on the A string.

So Ex. #8

It could also be played like this with a drone E:

Ex. #9

The better you prepare all of these musical examples, the faster you will learn the tune. When you feel ready, here is Part 1 with all of the variations we have worked on.

Lesson #4: Part 1 of Wake Up Susan with Variations

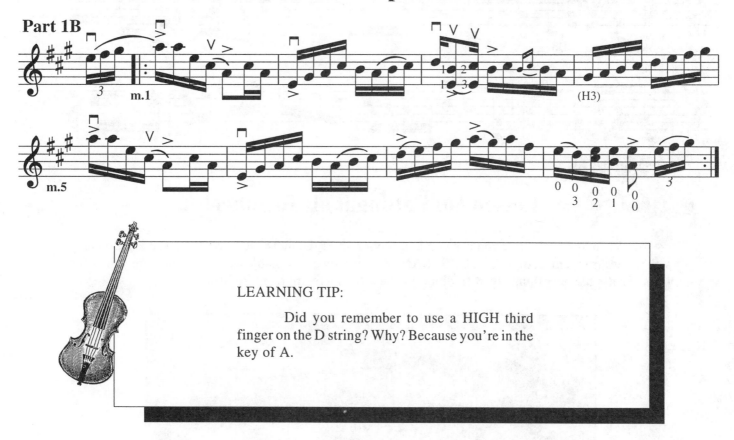

LEARNING TIP:

Did you remember to use a HIGH third finger on the D string? Why? Because you're in the key of A.

Lesson #5: Variations in Part 2 of Wake Up Susan

In Part 2 we can leave our notes the same, but by simply changing the rhythm ("doubling") the ear picks it up as really different.

So the old lick which sounded like:

Ex. #1

Will now sound like this:

Ex. #2

In measure 15 we will add one little extra note which will turn these notes into a triplet.

Ex. #3

So are you ready for the whole second part? Here it is!

Wake Up Susan - Part 2

Part 2B - Optional variation - (shuffle bowing)

Ex. #4

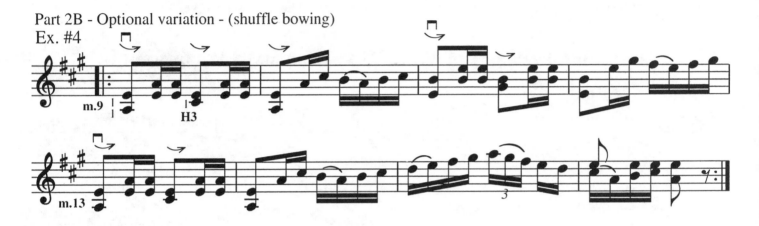

Lesson #6: Putting it all Together!

When you feel ready you can combine any or all of the ideas we have discussed and come up with a new arrangement of WAKE UP SUSAN. Mine is only one possible way. There are many possible ways. That's the neat thing about fiddling, the fact that there are many right ways!

One of the most wonderful bonuses of playing fiddle is the opportunity to meet and play with new friends. Here in this shot: Hanneke Cassel (1992, 1994 National Scottish Junior Fiddle Champion/1994, 1995 Oregon State Junior Fiddle Champion) of Port Orford, Oregon practices with Peter Willis of Pentleton, Oregon.

Lesson #6: Wake Up Susan
Arrangement #2

Key of A

Intro = 2 chops + 4 potatoes

Traditional
Arrangement by
Carol Ann Wheeler

Lesson #7: Whistler's Waltz

Sometimes when people think of fiddlers, they immediately think about playing fast and furious. The fact is, however, that fiddlers do play slow tunes. In the Scottish world fiddlers play beautiful expressive airs and laments. In the old-time fiddle world, they play waltzes. A waltz might be played to dance to, as one of the tunes in a contest set, or you can hear them being played just for listening pleasure at jam sessions.

Some fiddlers are happy learning and playing the standards (those tunes that everyone knows). In the Northwest, where I live, some real popular waltzes that everyone usually knows are: OVER THE WAVES, WESTPHALIA, and PEAKABOO (which you'll find in Vol. 1). Besides knowing the standards, I also enjoy learning other less-played tunes (sometimes called "off the wall"). The WHISTLER'S WALTZ I present here is one of that type of tune. Generally speaking, fiddle tunes usually have two parts. Every now and then you come across some that have three. "WHISTLER'S has three parts.

Years ago, I remember hearing Rusty Modrell (b. 1916-Idaho, d. 1995-Oregon) playing this waltz. He was one of the founding fathers of the Oregon Old Time Fiddlers and a great swing and old-time fiddler, that I admired. When I asked Rusty about the tune he said, "It was just this tune that this fellow used to whistle, so we called it Whistler's Waltz."

Let's play WHISTLER's with pretty much just the basic melody and using slides. Then I'll show you some of the ornaments and "fiddleydiddlies" I sometimes play.

Rusty Modrell
(1916-1995)

14

Lesson #7: Whistler's Waltz
Arrangement #1 - Basic Melody

Traditional
Arranged by
Carol Ann Wheeler

Key of D

Lesson #8: Ornaments and Variations Used in Whistler's Waltz

In our arrangement #2 of WHISTLER'S I have written out many of the ornaments and variations that I like to add. They have all been explained in Vol. 1 of CHILDREN'S FIDDLING METHOD. I will pull out a few for review before we try adding them in our final arrangement.

There are "flicks" used throughout as in measure 2

Ex. #1

I use "roll downs" as in measure 9.

Ex. #2

And I love "roll ups" as in measure 19.

Ex. #3

At measure 22-24 is a spot where I enjoy adding those "drone" strings we discussed in WAKE UP SUSAN.

At the end of this phrase, the last beat of measure 24, I changed the one A note into a "roll up."

Ex. #4

If you like the "roll up" sound, it might be a good idea to just pull it out and do some practice on it. You want it to sound clean with nimble fingers.

At measure 35 we have that good old "drone A" or double A that is so much a part of the fiddle sound.

Ex. #5

When I return to Part 1 at the end of WHISTLER'S, I really think of what I play as a *variation* and not so much ornamentation. It would be fine if you wanted to just play Part 1 again like the original. Remember, you do not *have* to do every single decoration just like me. It is fine to chose which ones you want for your collection.

Lesson #8: Whistler's Waltz
Arrangement #2 - With Ornaments and Variations

Traditional
Arrangement by
Carol Ann Wheeler

Key of D

Lesson #9: Katy Hill
Slides Preparation

One of the wonderful features of fiddling is that versions of the same tune will change or vary with each fiddler. I learned this arrangement of KATY HILL from James B. Herd (b. 1919-Missouri) of Sunnyside, Washington. I have always enjoyed Jim Herd's fiddling and thought there was a special touch to it. I think it is not only his personal fiddling but these particular arrangements that have a certain magic, old-timey feeling to them. Jim tells me that these tunes date way back to 1825 and that they have been played by fiddlers in his family since that time. These tunes have brought me lots of good luck in old-time-style fiddle contests. But once you learn the notes, please remember one of my most important "golden rules":

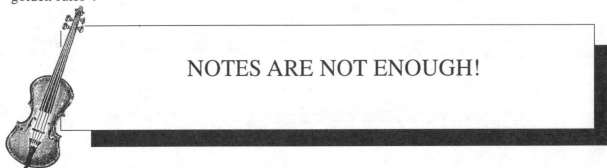

NOTES ARE NOT ENOUGH!

What this means is that merely playing the notes of a tune as written is not enough. You need that old time pulse. Listen to your recording. The trick is in the rhythm, slides, and accenting. With time you can use a little "test" that I like to do; watch your audience as you are playing. Can you see feet tapping? Fingers moving? Heads bobbing? That's what you're striving for, to make your audience respond to the pulse and heart beat of your fiddle!

4th Finger Slides

Sliding with the fourth finger is an important feature to this tune to give a special flavor. Practicing these slides will help prepare us. First do just a simple fourth finger slide on the E string:

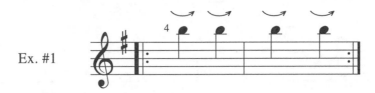

Ex. #1

Remember that a slide is made by placing the finger about a half inch below the written note and then sliding up into the note. Be careful not to slide past the note. You should be able to have different speeds of slides (slow and fast). Listen to your recording and you will hear my style. Listen to other fiddlers and you will hear other styles.

The other fourth finger slide involves two strings. I call it a drone E or Double E:

Ex. #2

You slide into your fourth finger on the A string and at the same time play your open E string (producing two E notes at the same time).

Advanced Lick – A Drone with a Flick

In example #3 we add one more thing to example #2, a quick little grace note or "flick" as I call it, with your second finger on the E string. It is important to do this second finger flick WITH THE FOURTH FINGER STILL *DOWN* AND STILL SOUNDING at the same time.

Ex. #3

If this is a new skill for you, you will probably find it challenging, in fact even frustrating! So please put your trust in me: Don't give up! This fiddle technique is worth any effort you invest in it. It is such a wonderful sound, one of the most important skills to add to your bag of tricks. Be kind to yourself and give yourself time to acquire this skill. It will be worth it!

Now the preparation on slides we have just done prepares us to try our first arrangement of KATY HILL.

Lesson #10: Katy Hill
Arrangement #1 - Basic Tune

Key of G
Intro: 2 "drags" + 4 potatoes

Lesson #11: Katy Hill (The Way I Play It)

Arrangement #2 - With Ornaments

Now we won't really be changing the tune much, but simply adding a few little "fiddleydiddlies."
I think they add so much to the flavor of this old tune. Also in my introduction, I like the sound of a D
(3rd finger on the A string) instead of the note B. It is more difficult, I think, but I really like this sound.
You can choose whichever sound you like.

Key of G

Intro: 2 drags + 4 potatoes

Traditional
Arranged by
Carol Ann Wheeler

LEARNING TIP:

About the rhythm: As you learn KATY HILL, and listen to your recording,
notice that there are spots in the music where I take liberties with the rhythm.
For example, there will be several spots where I come in a little early
(anticipation). This is difficult to notate in music, but something that you
can acquire by listening to your recording and playing along with me. Again
I feel this is something that really adds to that old-time-fiddle flavor.

20

Lesson #12: Something New! A Bonus! Twin Fiddle!

You have come so far since we used TWINKLE, TWINKLE LITTLE STAR to learn fiddle techniques back in Volume 1. So here is a fun bonus – something brand new for you, the chance to learn about twin fiddle! Some of the tunes in this volume will have harmony parts offered. If you do not care to do any twin fiddle at this time, the regular fiddle parts are just great played alone.

I have mentioned many times how much fun you can have playing with other musicians. You can jam with other fiddles, guitars, banjos, piano, bass, etc. Another way to enjoy your fiddle is to play twin fiddle with another fiddle player.

When two fiddle players play the same tune together, it is jamming. When two fiddlers play the same tune, but one plays the melody and the other the harmony, then it is *twin fiddling.*

BE SURE TO REVIEW THESE TIPS from time to time.

LEARNING TIPS ON TWIN FIDDLE:

1) It is very important that you each know your parts very well before beginning to practice together. The slightest pause or hesitation can throw the timing off.

2) It is good to practice just the two fiddle parts together first before adding backup.

3) The one who is playing lead (the first part) usually starts the tune.

4) It is important that you don't play too fast for your partner.

5) "Body language" is important. *Look* at each other at beginnings, endings, and other special parts of the tune. This is how you communicate.

6) Think of yourself as part of a team. You are not a soloist, the *team* together is the soloist.

7) When you first start playing with a twin partner, hearing harmony can be very exciting for you. Sometimes it can even mix you up and even throw you off. Practice slowly in the beginning. You will get used to hearing notes that are different than what you are playing, and with time you will develop the ability to listen to yourself and your twin-fiddle partner *at the same time.* This will be the real joy, the two fiddles playing in harmony.

To help us ease into twin fiddling, let's take a popular old two step that my daughter Tiffany and I used to play together when she was growing up. GOLDEN SLIPPERS was written in 1878 by an African-American banjo player, James A. Bland. One can only guess how many pioneers have played, sang, and danced to this tune...and it is still being played by fiddlers today.

Lesson #13: Golden Slippers (Two Step)
Arrangement #1

Key of G
Intro = 2 chops

James A. Bland (1854-1911)
Arranged by Carol Ann Wheeler

Lesson #14: Golden Slippers – Twin Fiddle Part
Arrangement #1

Now here's one possible twin-fiddle part. A practice technique that I find very helpful when creating and practicing harmony parts is to tape one part on my tape recorder, then play it back and *play along* with it (the other part not on the tape). Earphones can be helpful. You can play along with yourself on a tape recorder. Or when you feel ready, you can play along with me on your *learning recording* that goes along with this book.

Key of G
Intro = 2 chops

Lesson #15: Optional Additional Ideas for Golden Slippers

I chose GOLDEN SLIPPERS for our very first twin because it is a fairly simple tune, and I thought you would already be familiar with the melody. If you do not choose to play the twin part at this time, that's okay, but I really encourage you to try arrangement #2 as it has some nice "fiddlelydiddlelies" in it. You can use these same ideas in other tunes. All I did was add a few double stops and some turnarounds. Do you remember "turnarounds" from Volume 1 (Lesson 62)? They have been added at measures 2, 6, 9, and 14 in Part 1.

Lesson #16: Twin Fiddle to Golden Slippers
With Optional Ideas Added

The same ideas that we used to dress up our GOLDEN SLIPPERS are used in the twin-fiddle part. It is really a great sound when two fiddlers are doing the same "fiddlelydiddlelies" at the same time. Be sure to give accents to the last two notes of the tune. This will help to give it a feeling of really *ending*.

Golden Slippers - Twin Fiddle
Arrangement #2

Key of G
Intro. = 2 chops

Lesson #17: Preparing for TENNESSEE GRAY EAGLE

This is another Jim Herd tune dating back to 1825. I love playing this tune in my shows. I often look out into the audience and see tapping feet, bobbing heads, and smiles. When I have played it in "old-time contests," I have felt like I had a "secret weapon" as the tune itself seems to have an inner heartbeat.

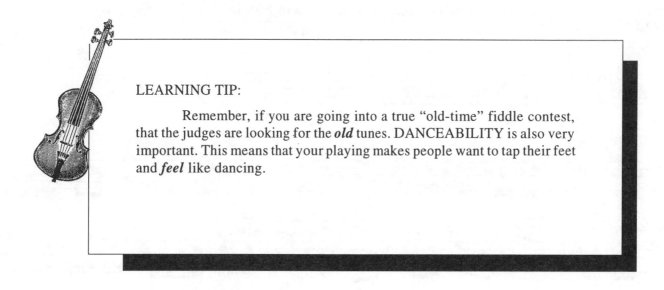

LEARNING TIP:

Remember, if you are going into a true "old-time" fiddle contest, that the judges are looking for the *old* tunes. DANCEABILITY is also very important. This means that your playing makes people want to tap their feet and *feel* like dancing.

TENNESSEE GRAY EAGLE has two parts. Like most fiddle tunes, one is high and one is low.

TENNESSEE GRAY EAGLE is in the key of C. If you do not feel comfortable with the finger patterns in the key of C, please return to your Vol. 1 of CHILDREN'S FIDDLING METHOD (Lesson #53) for a review of those finger patterns.

We use a "fat finger" (f.f.) a lot in the first part of TENNESSEE GRAY EAGLE so let's work on this technique.

Ex. #1

Since we are in the key of C, our shave (ending tag) will also be in C. It would be a good idea to work on this shave, so the ending will be up to the tempo of the tune when we come to the tune's end.

Ex. #2

Shave

(play at frog)

Lesson #18: Let's play Tennessee Gray Eagle

Arrangement #1

With that little bit of preparation done, we are now ready to play the whole tune. As soon as you feel comfortable with the notes, try playing along with me on the recording. This time you will also hear the twin fiddle part from lesson #20.

Key of C
Intro = 2 drags + 4 potatoes

Traditional
Arrangement by
Carol Ann Wheeler

LEARNING TIP:

Listening to a tune repeatedly on your recording *before* learning the tune will speed up the learning process!

On a sunny morning in June '91, Jim Herd and I jammed at the National Old-Time Fiddle Contest, held each year in Weiser, Idaho. Little did we know that later that evening he would win National Senior Senior Fiddle Champion. This is a division for fiddlers 70 years of age on up. There is also a Senior division for fiddlers 60-69 years of age.

Lesson #19: Optional Harmony to Tennessee Gray Eagle

Here is a twin-fiddle part to TENNESSEE GRAY EAGLE. Maybe you have a friend you could play with? Or perhaps you might play twin fiddle with your teacher or a parent?

LEARNING TIPS - for the harmony part:

1) At measure 27 we have a new fat finger (f.f.) set of finger patterns. We use the third finger on two strings at the same time. Since for most of us we need to turn our finger more on its side (where there are little pads of "fat"), I refer to it as the "fat finger" technique.

2) If you and your twin partner decide to add any of the optional bonus ideas from Lesson #21 to your arrangement, the "hippidy-hop" in example #2 works very well. This is where the body language of looking at each other comes in. What Linda (my twin-fiddle partner) and I do is to agree where we *want* the "hippidy-hop." Since I often forget to concentrate and sometimes do not put it in when I am supposed to, we back it up with our eyes (our body language). We look at each other, and I also give a little nod with my fiddle and my body. This tells Linda, "Here's the hippidy-hop *NOW!*" She watches me like a hawk, knows I didn't forget, and we play it *right together,* just as we planned!

James B. Herd of Sunnyside, Washington.

Lesson #20: Tennessee Gray Eagle – Twin Fiddle Part
Arrangement #1

Key of C

Lesson #21: Optional Bonus Ideas for Tennessee Gray Eagle

Our arrangement #1 of TENNESSEE GRAY EAGLE in Lesson #13 was a fine arrangement. It could serve a person their whole life. Sometimes, however, different fiddlers might add their own little touch to a tune after playing it over a period of time. Here are a few that I have added through the years. Listen to your learning recording and see if you like any of the ideas or licks I show you here. If you love the sound of something in fiddling and are willing to work for it, then it's just a matter of time before it's yours!

LEARNING TIP:

Always strive for QUALITY. Don't sacrifice quality for speed. If you have quality, then you can build speed over a period of time.

Our first bonus lick I nicknamed the "hippidy-hop." It involves measure 4. After I have played this musical idea several times (because it is a very predominate idea), I want to change from it and so I came up with simply changing the rhythm and repeating the notes. It's kind of like the idea of "doubling." When teaching this tune I like to stress that this was not part of the original tune as I learned it, so I always make sure to play the original several times first, before coming in with the "hippidy-hop." In fact, most of the time I wait until about the end, then put it in – kind of like a little surprise.

This was the original lick in measure 4

Ex. #1

This is the "hippidy-hop" lick I sometimes add towards the end of the tune to add a little something new.

Ex. #2

I also like adding a ♭ note (a first finger on the A string) to make a double stop on this same lick to give it a fuller sound.

Ex. #3

Of course, this same double stop also can be added to our "hippidy-hop" lick.

Ex. #4

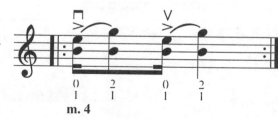

30

Lesson #22: Optional Bonus Licks for the 2nd part
of Tennessee Gray Eagle

There have been times when I was playing a tune that my bow accidently bumped a string (a mistake). Sometimes I found that I liked that sound, so I decided to sometimes "plan" on playing that string on purpose.

In the second part of TENNESSEE GRAY EAGLE, there are several opportunities to have an open string "droning." It's not difficult to do; it's simply a matter of saying to yourself, "I am going to play two strings here...and here," and then do it.

Part 2 - With open "drone" strings

Now really give a "pull" with your bow when playing these "drone" open strings, especially the G string, to set it in motion so it will ring for a while.

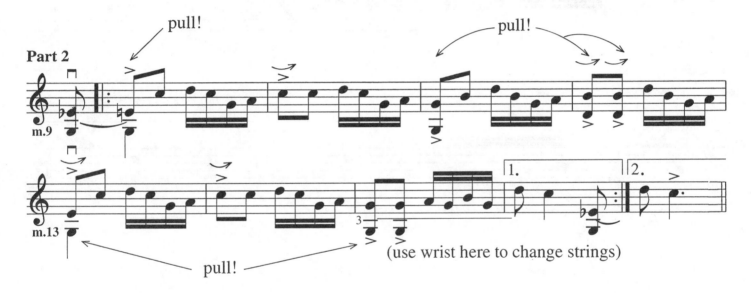

Lesson #23: Using "hokum" bowing in the 2nd part

There is that style of bowing called "hokum," which is considered trick fiddling or show fiddling. One of my students (John Waddingham of Portland, Oregon) came up with the idea of using it in the second part. I loved the idea and began using it in my shows. It made the tune into a show tune, and gave some nice variety. "Hokum" is a tricky style of bowing. If you do not already know it, it will probably take some work on your part. Listening to your learning recording will help a lot. If you have a tape recorder that has one of those slow speeds, listen to the hokum on slow speed. Pay close attention to the accents. They are one of the secrets to success on hokum bowing.

LEARNING TIP:

Never play hokum bowing in a standard fiddle contest. You could be eliminated. Hokum is great for trick or novelty contests.

Tennessee Gray Eagle - Part 2 Using Hokum Bowing

LEARNING TIPS on hokum bowing:

✔ Did you notice the irregular patterns? Like how you play on the bottom pair of strings *twice,* then on the middle pair of strings only *once*? This pattern is repeated five times.

✔ Did you notice that you put accents on the upper pair of notes? Getting the *accents* correct is very important to getting the real "feel" to hokum.

✔ Having a *flexible wrist* will help you in getting that special "punch" in hokum. "Whip" that wrist!

Lesson #24: Bonus Hokum Pattern –offered for Advanced Students

Part 2 – Tennessee Gray Eagle

If you have the hokum down pat and enjoy the sounds of the show fiddling, here's a little bonus for you. It's a little variation in the bowing pattern of the hokum. I do not change the notes. I simply change the way I bow them so the fingers will not be doing the work; it will be the bow arm doing the work.

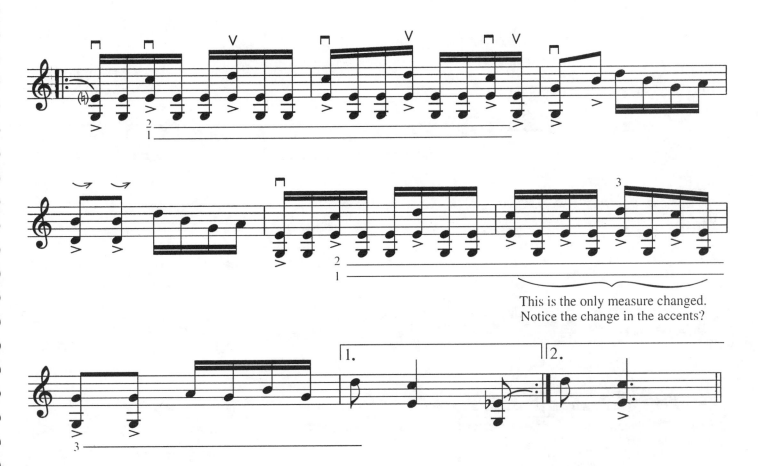

This is the only measure changed. Notice the change in the accents?

Twelve-year-old Jason Barlow of Hillsboro, Oregon really has fun playing fiddle. He belongs to a Bluegrass band made up of young musicians. Jason enjoys adding TENNESSEE GRAY EAGLE to many of his fiddle shows.

33

Lesson #25: A Show Arrangement of Tennessee Gray Eagle

If you have learned TENNESSEE GRAY EAGLE in Lesson #18, I am proud of you! If you choose to play that arrangement that is just fine. For those of you who really enjoy this fine old tune and wish for a longer version, we will put together the ideas we learned in lessons #21, 22, 23, and 24 to create a longer, more complicated show version. If you do not quite feel ready for this longer version, it's OK to set it aside and you can come back at a later time when you feel more ready for it.

Tennessee Gray Eagle
Arrangement #2

Traditional
Arranged by
Carol Ann Wheeler

Part 2 - With Hokum Bowing

Lesson #26: The Bullfrog Blues

I love to play this next tune! It's a swingy little blues tune called "The Bullfrog Blues." I have played it in old-time contests and dance contests, and audiences enjoy it during shows.

"Bullfrog" is in the key of F, which has B♭ in it. It would be a good idea for us to review the finger patterns in F. Let's do that by playing an F scale.

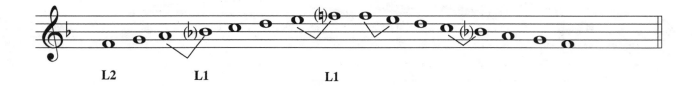

Did you remember to play a *low* first finger on the A and E strings?

BULLFROG BLUES is one of those "off-the-wall" tunes, so not everyone is going to know it. I think it's terrific to play something a little different. You need to have a pretty fair guitar player as the key of F is a bit challenging for some.

LEARNING TIP:

When you play in a standard fiddle contest, you play a hoedown, then a waltz, and finally a tune of choice.

Tune of choice means the fiddler has some choices: They could choose a rag, polka, schottiche, jig, two step, clog, or a blues. All of these tunes are types of dances. A fiddler could *not* choose to play another hoedown or waltz. You could use BULLFROG BLUES as a tune of choice.

Optional Twin Part

In Lesson #27 you will find the optional twin fiddle part to the BULLFROG BLUES. This is being shared by my twin fiddle partner of about 19 years, Linda Danielson of Eugene, Oregon. Playing twin fiddle with Linda through the years has been one of the many joys of playing fiddle. I hope you will have a good friend that you might play BULLFROG with, too.

A FROG'S TALE

– – o – –

by Jim Lattig, 1969

One time into a pail of cream
    two little froggies fell,
At first it was a lot of fun,
    they swam for quite a spell.

And when they wearied of the sport,
    they tried to find a place
Where they could rest themselves
    for just a little space.

But resting places for two frogs
    in all this creamy pail –
Alas – they found were just as scarce
    as any froggy's tail.

"I'm done, I'm done," one froggy cried
    and sank beneath the cream
The other frog swam on and on
    to carry out his scheme.

The more he swam, the more he churned
    up chunks of butterfat,
Until he'd churned a pound or two,
    then climbed upon the pat.

And used it for a launching pad
    to leave this creamy pail,
And that, precisely, is the point,
    the moral of this tale:

Whenever you are faced by odds,
    that seem to have you licked,
Remember how the frog survived
    because he kicked and kicked.

– – x – –

My Uncle Jim (a fiddler, b. 1908-Missouri, d. 1990-Illinois), made up this poem about a frog. It kind of has the same philosophy about life that I have had about fiddling, and that is not to give up. Many years ago, when I first started learning to play fiddle, some people told me I wouldn't be able to play fiddle. I didn't give up, and I did a lot of kicking. If you love fiddle, that's the important thing. Just keep working and kicking, and you'll learn to play, too!

37

Lesson #26: Bullfrog Blues

39

Lesson #27: Bullfrog Blues – Optional Twin Fiddle

Arrangement by
Linda Danielson

40

Lesson #28: Marmaduke's Hornpipe
Preparing for Arrangement #1

Get ready, here comes one of my favorites! This is a great old-time square dance tune with a very danceable beat...a kind of built-in pulse! It was one of the tunes that my daughter Tiffany (at that time 11 years old) played in 1982 when she won National Jr. Jr. Fiddle Champion. It has been one of my favorite tunes to play in old-time fiddle contests. In this version, there are lots of double strings, giving it a thick sound.

Let's take a look at the first part to prepare ourselves for the tune. Notice that we have the fat finger technique used a lot. Also notice that we do a pattern, then we repeat that same pattern but alter the timing a little. It's the bow that is doing most of the work, and not so much the fingers.

Ex. #1

In Part 2, we begin with a "roll-up" to "D" on the A string.

Then we add *to this* "D" an "F♯" on the E string.

Please remember to *leave down* your third finger as you add the F♯ to it. I really like to "milk" this first finger slide. You can hear this on your learning recording.

Ex. #2

Next, we'll add the next measure, m. 10, which is where we "bobble" our bow. (Remember from Vol. 1, Lesson #19, where the bow "bobbles" back and forth from one string to another?)

Ex. #3

With that little bit of preparation, we are ready to try our first arrangement of MARMADUKE'S HORNPIPE.

Lesson #29: Marmaduke's Hornpipe
Arrangement #1

Traditional
Arranged by
Carol Ann Wheeler

Key of D

Intro. = 2 chops + 4 potatoes

Lesson #30: Optional Harmony Part to Marmaduke's

Here's the optional harmony part for MARMADUKE'S arrangement #1. MARMADUKE'S makes a great twin fiddle tune.

There's one measure in Part 2 of the tune where you have some rapid finger movement on the E string of a low one to a high one. They are triplet sixteenth-notes so they move right along. I've written them out here so that you can make them into a little exercise to work on them.

Play this measure slowly, then build your technique by repeating several times, gradually building speed. When you reach *your* limit and begin to sound sloppy, DO NOT PLAY ANY FASTER. Drop back down to a tempo where you can play with quality.

LEARNING TIP:

Removing those measures from a tune which are tricky for you and making them into little practice exercises as we just did above, is a SUPER practice technique. It is a SECRET WEAPON to getting better on your fiddle. I call it the "broken record technique" because you take a lick and repeat it over and over and over. In my life, I have observed countless fiddlers who practice a tune all of the time at the same speed. That's it! And they never seem to get any better. Now you know why.

BONUS TWIN FIDDLE PART FOR ADVANCED STUDENTS

When you listen to Lesson #33, you will also hear a twin fiddle part. The second fiddle mimics what is being played in the first fiddle. It is simply using the same ideas (as explained in Lesson #32) for measure 3 (and 7) and measure 4. Only two measures are changed (in the repeat of part 1), but it really changes the whole sound of this repeat.

For those of you that really like this sound, here are those two measures written out.

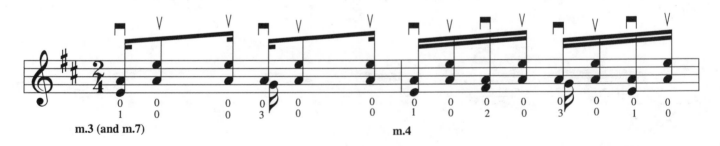

SECRET! You are HOW you practice!

To get better
USE GOOD PRACTICE TECHNIQUES!

Lesson #31: Optional Harmony to Marmaduke's Hornpipe
Arrangement #1

Key of D

Intro = 2 chops + 4 potatoes

Ending Tag

SPECIAL NOTE: If you enjoyed the TWIN fiddle part for MARMADUKE'S HORN-PIPE, arrangement #1, but feel ready for the challenge of a longer version, study over the preparation notes in lesson #32. You and your twin fiddle partner can add any of these variations to your arrangement that you like (see page 44).

Lesson #32: More Ideas and Variations
for Marmaduke's Hornpipe

Our arrangement #1 is a fine version of MARMADUKE'S HORNPIPE. If you love this tune like I do, I am sure you'll want to add these great variations. They add so much!

In Part 1 there is a perfect place to use the "drone A" or "double A."

Of course, you'll want to slide *into* these double "A's," play two of them, then "let go" with your fourth finger and continue the tune as you know it. I absolutely *love* this sound! If you do too, listening to your learning recording will help you capture it.

Ex. #1

Ex. #1

I love the sound of this next variation! It's in the "fat finger" section (measures 3 and 4). We can nickname it the "hippidy-hop." Plus we add some bow bobble.

Here is how it is written. Be sure to listen to your listening recording. It will help you. Notice the special bowing I use: down up, up down up, up...etc.

Ex. #2

"Bow Bobble"

Right here in measure 4, a flexible wrist is really important.

At measure 16 is a spot where occasional variations will help prevent monotony. Adding some variety can be accomplished so easily! USE THE SAME NOTES. Just CHANGE THE RHYTHM!

Different Ways to Play the Same Measure

Ex. #3 - The original
Last measure

Ex. #4 - One Variation
A nice long "drag"

Ex. #5 - Another Variation
A little fancier

All of these ideas can be used in other tunes that you know.

National Fiddle Contest - Weiser, Idaho - 1982

| Heather Kolbreck | Trisha Brown | Tiffany Wheeler | Linnete Lane | Chad Ruwe | Michele Eisle |
| Minnesota | California | Oregon | California | Idaho | Washington |

One of the wonderful pluses of playing fiddle is meeting and making friends from other states. My children and I made lots of friends and pen pals that we have kept for years. We all look forward to the contests not just for playing our fiddles, but for getting to see our friends. Here in this shot you can see how many different states are represented. After the contests they'd all be running and playing together out on the camp ground.
(Photo by Stark Photography)

Lesson #33: Marmaduke's Hornpipe
Arrangement #2 – Using Variations

Traditional
Arranged by
Carol Ann Wheeler

Key of D
Intro. = 2 chops + 4 potatoes

Lesson #34: Preparation for Bear Creek Hop!

"BEAR CREEK HOP!" is a fun little show tune that I learned from Rusty Modrell (b. 1916-Idaho, d. 1995-Oregon) of Oregon. We were performing at a fair in the summer, and the crowd started chanting to Rusty, "Bear Creek Hop! Bear Creek Hop!...Bear Creek Hop!" So Rusty smiled and played it. The crowd loved it, and I made up my mind I wanted to learn to play it. I asked Rusty if he'd share it with me, and I would then pass it on to many other fiddlers. Rusty was happy about that.

A show tune is a tune that you play to entertain at shows. Often times, show tunes will have some special trick fiddling in them. It is important to remember, boys and girls, when playing in a standard fiddle contest, it is probably *not* a good idea to do show tunes. In BEAR CREEK HOP! we have some left-hand pizzicato, and pizzicato is definitely considered novelty or trick fiddling. It could get you eliminated (if played in a standard contest). It is okay, however, in a "no-rules" contest.

Let's Get Started!

To prepare, let's practice the left hand pizzicato. In the music you will see this is indicated by a "+" mark. This left-hand pizzicato is just like the pizzicato we learned in Vol. 1 (Lesson #63 for "BOIL THE CABBAGE"), so if you have learned it in Vol. 1 it will be easier for you now.

With your third finger, pluck the "A" and "E" strings, then follow it with bowing the same open notes.

Be sure you are at the frog.

Ex. #1

 Notice that you do "pluck, bow, pluck, bow," and that one time you use a *down* bow and then next an *up* bow. Your arm swings back and forth and has a kind of bounce to it.

Other than the pizzicato, everything else in BEAR CREEK is pretty standard. Go ahead and get familiar with the notes. You will find it on your learning recording played slowly.

If you love this tune like I do, you want to memorize it right away. When you get your eyes away from reading the music, you will then begin to get some speed. And speaking of "speed," here is a neat little trick I do that I want to share with you. It's a bonus for you speed demons.

BONUS PERFORMANCE TIP:

To create a feeling of EXCITEMENT!

The last time I play through the first part, I like to speed up the tempo. Usually I double it. Be sure to warn your backup that you plan to do this. And you'll need to use a lot of body language to keep your back up with you. Look at them just before you change the tempo.

Lesson #34: Bear Creek Hop!

Lesson #35: Preparation for Roy's Rag

Our next tune could be used in a fiddle contest as a "tune of choice." The third tune in an American fiddle contest is a variety tune and must be something other than another hoedown or waltz. ROY'S RAG was made up in 1960 by Roy Bredy of Creston, B.C. Our family really enjoyed this tune and in 1981 when we produced our second fiddle album, Roy gave us permission to include his Rag on the album. Tiffany, then 10 years old, played the lead, and I played second fiddle. It was one of Tiffany's favorite "tune of choice." Roy must have loved Cajun fiddling, for you can surely hear its influence in ROY'S RAG. It would also be a great tune to play at a dance, and audiences love it.

"Rags" have a dotted rhythm or feel to them. Let's first get a little comfortable with this rhythm by playing the following exercises, which is actually just the first three measures:

Ex. #1
measure 1, 3, 3

Now notice that this next pattern or lick, looks totally different. When you really stop to think about it, you realize that you use the same fingers as Ex. #1, but now they are played on the D string, and the pattern is played only two times instead of three.

Ex. #2
measure 5 & 6

LEARNING TIP:

Remember that "patterns" are very helpful when learning and playing a tune.

At measure 30 as we are ending Part 1, we have a little chromatic lick. We play a regular one on the "A" string (the note B), and then slide our regular one to a LOW one (B♭) and then right back up to regular one.

Practice this lick, measure 30, until you can play it very smoothly. Try to *feel* "Hey, this is easy!" When you play it, make it sound EASY!

Ex. #3

We just have a couple more pieces of homework to do before we are ready to play ROY'S RAG. You are doing great! Remember, the better you can play these little exercises, the better you will play the finished tune!

There are some slides in ROY'S RAG, a lot of second finger slides.

First there is a low two on the "E" string. Remember, to slide on this note you need to put your second finger **on** "F♯" and slide **up** to the note "G."

Ex. #4

m.35 L2

Then we have some high twos - in fact, four of them.

Ex. #5

m.37 H2

It might be a good idea to work on our ending a little. Upon closer inspection, you will see that it is an "A" scale! Can you see the "A" scale in there?

Then after you play the "A" scale, you hang on to the three on the "E" string (the note A), and add a low 2 on the "A" (the note C♮) and then slide it **up** to a C♯. This is a real typical sound in fiddling, and one I really like.

(a scale)

Ex. #6

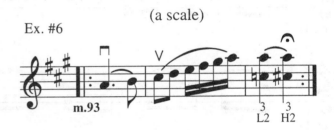

m.93

3   3
L2   H2

If this ending is too difficult for you now, you could play a nice long "A" and "E" string drone. Of course you'd want to keep working on the other ending. With practice, it's simply just a matter of time. DON'T GIVE UP!

Ex. #7

Optional Alternate Easy Ending

m.93

1   L1   1

Here's that easier ending written out for you. Play this ending starting at m. 93 instead of the last four measures written (the "A scale ending") in arrangement #1. Or *you* could make up an ending yourself!

Now, I think we are ready to begin playing ROY'S RAG!

Lesson #36: Roy's Rag
Arrangement #1 - Using Single Strings

Key of A
Intro = 2 chops + 3 pickup notes

by Roy Bredy
Arrangement by Carol Ann Wheeler

Part 1

m. 1

m. 5

m. 11

m. 17

m. 21

Part 2

m. 25

m. 30

m. 33

m. 41

Lesson #37: Roy's Rag - Using Two Strings

After you are feeling comfortable playing ROY'S RAG on single strings, then you are ready for the "frosting on the cake" part. Don't worry! It's not too hard for you! But wow! Is it going to make a big difference in your sound! You will sound *fuller,* because you are playing on *two* strings at the same time.

Here's how it works:

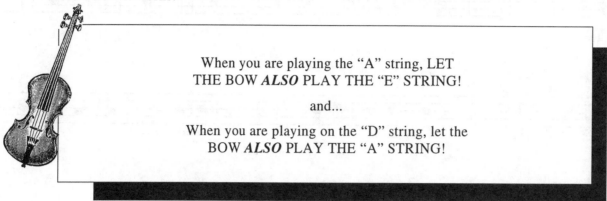

When you are playing the "A" string, LET THE BOW *ALSO* PLAY THE "E" STRING!

and...

When you are playing on the "D" string, let the BOW *ALSO* PLAY THE "A" STRING!

That's all there is to it! It is simply a matter of setting your mind to it. Your brain is in charge of telling your body *what* to do. In fiddling, your brain is very important.

The only exception to this rule is at measure 35. I don't think the G♯ on the "E" string sounds good with an open "A" string, so we will need to play the note "B" here (a one on the "A" string). Here is that one little section written out for you (in case you'd like to practice it!) in preparation for our next arrangement.

Ex. #1

The reason I didn't show you the music to ROY'S RAG (on two strings) right in the beginning is that I personally feel it looks pretty busy. In fact, if I am really honest with you, it kind of looks a little scary to me and I didn't want it to scare you.

You could play arrangement #1, plus "set your mind" as I have explained to you. Or you can play this next arrangement #2, which has all of the open drone strings written out for you in the music.

Okay, now you can look at the music. But remember - don't let it intimidate or scare you!

Fiddlers and Friends

This group of young fiddlers decided on their own to get a group shot while at the National Fiddlers Contest held always the third full week in June annually. For many fiddlers, seeing old friends at the contests is just as important as the contest. (Back row: Scott Ranes of Oregon, Stacey Adair of Idaho, Sherry West of Oregon, Grant Wheeler of Oregon. Front row: Tiffany Wheeler, Andrea Vogt of Idaho, Amy Ranes of Oregon.) - Photo by Stark

Lesson #37: Roy's Rag
Arrangement #2 - On Two Strings

Key of A
Intro = 2 chops + 3 pick up notes

by Roy Bredy
Arrangement by
Carol Ann Wheeler

Lesson #38: Optional Harmony to Roy's Rag

Here is one possible harmony part to ROY'S RAG. It will work with arrangement #1 or #2. To play as written you need to feel comfortable with using the "fat-finger" technique and double stops. If you really want to play the harmony but aren't quite ready to play both double stops, you can leave out the top note in the double stop. Also, very important: you and your twin will want to talk it over and agree on your overall rhythm. Will you choose to accent all the way through *ON THE BEAT?* Or will you go for the true Cajun flavor by accenting on the *OFF BEAT?*

LEARNING TIP:

Rhythm is very important to the sound of ROY'S RAG. You and your twin fiddle partner will want to put accents in the same places. Like at measure 39, there is a tasty syncopated accent on the off beat that you will want to talk about. You should agree to really *lean* on this note, and when you come to it, be sure to look at each other. This is your signal to one another saying, "Let's give a good PUSH here!"

Lesson #38: Optional Harmony to Roy's Rag

Key of A
Intro = 2 chops + pick up

Arranged by Carol
Ann Wheeler

Roy's Rag - harmony continued

61

Lesson #39: Contemporary Fiddle Tunes

For the most part, our tunes in Volumes 1 and 2 of CHILDREN'S FIDDLING METHOD have been old tunes – some of them close to 200 years old. They are usually called traditional tunes. They have been around so long that no one really knows for sure who made them up. ROY'S RAG in Lesson #36 is different because it was made up by someone who lives in contemporary times. You see, boys and girls, old-time fiddle music is still being written. One-hundred years from now the tunes being written today will be considered old. I think it is wonderful to know a lot of the old tunes, but I also think it is terrific to learn new, fresh tunes. It is fun to pull out something new and different at jams and shows.

Our next tune, MY COUSIN'S REEL, was written by my twin fiddle partner, Linda Danielson of Eugene, Oregon. Linda had sent me a tape with a whole group of new tunes for us to try for twin fiddle. One tune especially caught my ear the most, but there was no name for it. When I asked her the name, Linda said, "It doesn't have one." Later I found out that Linda had written it. She wrote it for her cousin as a Christmas present, and that's how the name came about. It is in "B" minor and a totally different style than any of the other tunes in this volume. I love the tune, and it's really fun to play! Linda said, "It just came bubbling out!" That's how I feel about the tune when I play it, a kind of "bubbling feeling" which is created by a lot of string crossing.

MY COUSIN'S REEL is a contra dance tune, the old-time-style dance from New England. Contra dance is popular today with folk dancing groups. When Linda and I recorded our "Joy of Twin Fiddling" album, we played MY COUSIN'S REEL in a medley.

Preparing for MY COUSIN'S REEL

There is quite a bit of rapid string crossing in this tune, especially in the second part. A nice flexible wrist will be a real help. Here's an exercise that is easy to do that will help you focus on your wrist.

The Wrist Exercise

INSTRUCTIONS: You will repeat the exercise at least three times, thinking of your strings as "pairs." For example, the G and D are the bottom pair, the D and A the middle pair.

Begin playing slowly, using big bows, gradually increasing the speed, using smaller bows as you gain speed. Use an indefinite number of notes (refer to recording).

Ex. #1

Ex. #2

Ex. #3 - Repeat the wrist exercise on the top pair of strings.

Wrist - CHECK OFF LIST

✔ • **Look** – Actually look at your wrist both directly (your eye looking at your arm) and indirectly by looking in the mirror (your eye looks in a mirror at your arm).

✔ • **Think** – "Wrist relax!"

✔ •**Think** – "Hand drop...hand lift." You should see your right hand drop and lift.

✔ • **Realize** – That the bow will actually tilt as you lift and drop to change strings.

✔ •**Wrist! Not Arm!** – You change strings by using your wrist, not your arm.

✔ • **Bow Size** – Please remember to apply one of my golden rules when playing this exercise:

Golden Rule!

"The faster you go, the smaller you bow."

The wrist skill you gain from this exercise will help you in countless other fiddle tunes as well as MY COUSIN'S REEL.

If you enjoy and feel you could benefit from more exercises, there is a special method available called "Aerobics for Fiddlers!" published by Mel Bay.

Lesson #40: My Cousin's Reel
Arrangement #1

Key of B

Intro = one long "drag"

Linda L. Danielson

Lesson #41: Optional Twin Fiddle to My Cousin's Reel

I am delighted that my twin fiddle partner, Linda Danielson, has agreed to share her twin fiddle part to MY COUSIN'S REEL. Linda has a special gift for hearing harmony parts to fiddle tunes. Not all tunes are suitable for twin fiddle, but MY COUSIN'S REEL *is* a GREAT twin number!

Arrangement #1

Key of B
Intro = one long "drag"

Linda Danielson

Lesson #42: Optional Variations on My Cousin's Reel

MY COUSIN'S REEL is wonderful just as played in arrangement #1. When Linda and I recorded it, we agreed we both liked the variations as written here in the second part in arrangement #2. Upon a closer look you will realize that it is simply the use of "doubling" as we have discussed earlier. It only happens twice (in measures 26 and 28), but this causes the only two quarter-notes (the long notes where you would normally have a chance to "rest" a moment) to be changed into eighth-notes, making the whole second part a continuous movement. This is why Linda and I made up our own nickname for this particular variation of "continuous movement." You can use any of these ideas in your twin.

At measure 19 is the original way that Linda actually wrote the tune. You can compare this with the way I play measure 3 in our arrangement #1.

You can change the way you bow notes and it will change the sound! Notice this at measures 23 and 24, how it sounds different when you put in the slurs.

ENDING:

Did you notice that we used just a nice long "drag"? I feel that our "shave and a hair cut" style ending is simply out of character for this style of fiddling. It would be like wearing cowboy boots with a pretty prom dress. They just don't go together.

Carol Ann Wheeler and Linda Danielson, Oregon State Twin Fiddle Champions
My twin-fiddle partner and I have been friends and enjoyed playing together for almost 20 years. Fiddling is a great way to meet new friends.

Lesson #42: My Cousin's Reel
Arrangement #2 – With Variations

Key of B
Intro = one long "drag"

Linda L. Danielson
Arrangement by
Carol Ann Wheeler

Lesson #43: A New Key!

If you have played violin for a few years, you have probably already played in B♭. The key of B♭ is really no big deal. However, in the fiddle world I have noticed a peculiarity. Many fiddlers when they refer to B♭, talk like it's something hard and different and a mystery to them. I have noticed that fiddlers who have played many years in the open keys (G, D, A) and then tried B♭ sometimes had some difficulty. Where as I have seen students who have only played a couple of years try B♭ and have no problem. I came to the conclusion that those who had played for years in the open keys simply got used to those finger patterns, and anything else felt strange.

Here is a B♭ scale written out so you can get used to the finger patterns in B♭.

B♭ Scale

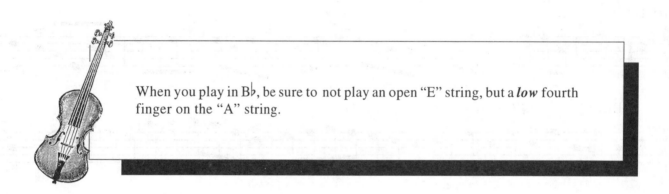

When you play in B♭, be sure to not play an open "E" string, but a *low* fourth finger on the "A" string.

Now we can use our B♭ playing skill to play one of my favorite waltzes, THE SATURDAY NIGHT WALTZ. I heard this years ago when playing in Canada and fell in love with it the very first time I heard it. I have had a lot of good luck with this waltz when I have played it in "old time" style contests, because it has such a great danceable rhythm. "LORDAGS VALSEN" was the original name of this Norwegian waltz. This translates to "Saturday Waltz," but Americans added the word "Night" to it. It was made up by Anselm Johannson in 1921, and was a favorite among Scandinavian-Americans during the 1920's and 1930's.

One of my "secrets" when I play this waltz is to put the "fat one" (a heavy emphasis on the first beat of every measure) throughout. This waltz already has great danceability, but the "fat one" brings it out even more. Listen to this danceability on your recording.

A group of Jr. Jr. Fiddlers (from Idaho, Montana, Washington, and Oregon) pose with their trophies at the Northwest Regional Fiddlers Contest at Spokane, Washington in 1982.

The Jr. Jr. was a division for children up to and including 12 years of age.

Today, Jr. Jr. divisions are for kids nine to twelve. A new division has been added to many state, regional, and national contests called the Small Fry or Pee Wee division. This was created for kids eight years old and under. It is absolutely unbelievable how well some of these young fiddlers can play!

Lesson #43: Saturday Night Waltz

by Anselm Johannson
Arranged by Carol
Ann Wheeler

Part 3 (play this section smoother)

Lesson #44: Preparing for Sandy River Belle

Usually fiddlers learn their tunes from other fiddlers, but SANDY RIVER BELLE is an Appalachian tune I learned from a banjo player. He played it in the key of "A," but I have heard that it is also played in "G."

In my arrangement, SANDY RIVER BELLE can be played on two strings throughout. I really like that sound for this tune. Our first arrangement, however, will be only on one string. This will help us to first get acquainted with the notes.

There is not nearly the shifting (to higher positions) in the fiddle world that there is in the violin world. For the banjo, the key of "A" was good, but for fiddlers it means in this arrangement that we need to shift (at measures 10 and 14) on the "E" string to reach a high C♯. If shifting is new to you, this little exercise will help you prepare for SANDY RIVER BELLE.

To SHIFT means that the hand moves up the neck of the fiddle in order to reach higher notes.

To shift in third position means:

Where you normally place your THIRD finger, you RE-PLACE it with your FIRST. *IMPORTANT* – Your WHOLE HAND "shifts" (moves-slides) up the neck of the fiddle. i.e. Take your thumb *along* (don't leave it back in first position).

Step 1:

First, let's practice "shifting" up to the third position.

We play up to the note "A," listen to it, then move (shift) our entire left hand UP the neck of the fiddle far enough to now be able to play that same "A" note with the *first* finger. We are now in the third position!

Step 2:

Now we will leave out the little scale and go more directly to the shift in Ex. #2 and then use this shift to reach our goal, that high C♯.

Step 3:

Now a little exercise that practices the actual notes in our tune. We shift from open E right to that high C♯. But now we should feel more comfortable, because now we know *where* we are going and *how* to get there.

Practice these exercises. Listen and play along with me on your learning recording.

When you feel prepared for the shifting, then you are ready for our first arrangement below.

Lesson #45: Sandy River Belle
Arrangement #1 - Single Strings

Traditional
Arrangement by
Carol Ann Wheeler

LEARNING TIP: TAG

Did you notice that we did not use a standard fiddle shave this time? To give variety I took a phrase from the tune and simply played it again. I think it gives a nice feeling of..."This *is* the end."

Lesson #46: Adding drone strings to "Sandy River Belle"

When you are learning the notes to a tune you have to *think* about which fingers to use. After you have practiced it a lot, then you get to a point I call the "secondary level." This is where you don't have to think about each and every finger. You "hear" the tune in your head and your fingers just go to where they are supposed to. This is a GREAT point to reach. It shows you are making progress!

When you feel comfortable with arrangement #1 and have reached the secondary level, then you can try adding the drones in arrangement #2. As in the past, when you are on the "A" string, let the "E" string sound. When you are on the "E" string, let the "A" string sound. When you are on the "D" string, let the "A" string sound. In this tune there will be something different, an exception to these rules:

At measure 12, I do not like the sound of an open "A" string here, so I play a one on the "A" string (a B note). This is a true double stop. It would be a good idea to practice this little exercise here, and then it will be much easier for you when you come to this in Part 2.

This is the one exception to using all open string drones in SANDY RIVER BELLE.

This lick really happens fast in the tune, so after you can play it by itself, practice the whole line of music where it occurs.

Ex. #2

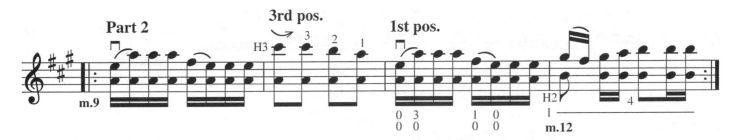

We have worked hard! Good for you. Let's have some fun now and add our drones to SANDY RIVER BELLE.

Lesson #46: Sandy River Belle
Arrangement #2 - On Two Strings

Traditional
Arrangement by
Carol Ann Wheeler

Lesson #47: Optional Bonus Ideas for Sandy River Belle for Advanced Students

Our arrangement #2 of SANDY RIVER BELLE is just fine. However, there are a couple more neat tricks that I do that I'd like to share with you. Listen to your learning recording, and if you like them, with just a little bit of work you can also do them.

Here's how they work:

ORNAMENTS: I like to put some "flicks" in. You can see them all written in the music. Feel free to chose the ones that *you* like.

DOUBLING: In Part 2 you will find some places (at measures 10, 12 and 14) where I give the tune more activity or movement through changing *one* note into *two* shorter notes.

RHYTHM: Notice the accent marks (>) on the off beat? It gives the tune a special, old-timey feel. We learned this technique (Lesson #2) in Volume 1. If you cannot automatically turn your inner drummer on to accenting on the off beats, then here is a little exercise for you to review that technique.

Ex. #1

TROUBLE WITH THE RHYTHM?

If you feel awkward with trying to accent on the off beat, please do not feel badly. It is just that it is new to you. I had trouble with this too in the beginning, but I just didn't give up.

Listen to your learning recording. Play the rhythm exercise slowly. Play the tune slowly. Give yourself time. It's worth the effort! It's a great sound. And you can use this technique in a lot of fiddle tunes to give them a special old-timey sound.

Lesson #47: Sandy River Belle
Arrangement #3 – With Ornaments and Off-Beat Accents

Traditional
Arrangement by Carol
Ann Wheeler

Intro = 2 drags + 4 potatoes

Lesson #48: Sandy River Belle - Twin Fiddle Part
Arrangement #1 - With Single Notes

I will give you two arrangements of the twin fiddle part for SANDY RIVER BELLE. Either of them will go with any of the first fiddle parts.

Here is arrangement #1, which is all with single notes.

Lesson #49: Sandy River Belle - Twin Fiddle Part
Arrangement #2 - With Double Stops

Arrangement #2 may be more of a challenge for you. It is totally played in double stops, but really gives a wonderfully thick, rich sound. It looks pretty busy when you first look at the music. Don't let is scare you off. If you love the sound of this twin fiddle part, give yourself some time to get used to it. In the beginning you'll need to go slowly and it may feel awkward. But what can happen on fiddle, if you give it some time, is your fingers begin to memorize the tune by *feel.* I call this kinesthetic memory or "muscle memory." This can happen over a period of time and it has helped me out of tight situations many times.

Arrangement #2 is actually arrangement #1 with double stops added. Most of the double stops are drones (open strings that ring as you play a note). There are also a lot of "fat finger" ones and one real double stop that happens several times. This real double stop is in the last measure, and it happens several times in Part 1.

Lesson #50: Preparing for My Wild Irish Rose

Here's a beautiful old waltz that touches the hearts of many listeners. My daughter Tiffany used to play this when she was 9, 10, and 11 years old. It was one of the waltzes she played in 1982 when she won National Jr. Jr. Fiddle Championship. It has some double stops in it that used to give her a hard time, so we spent lots of time working on them.

You'll need a good guitar player to play this waltz. I find that some guitar players shy away from "B♭."

Let's work just a little on some of the double stops to help make this tune easier for you. They occur in Part 2. (Practice extra on any that are difficult for you.)

First we play an F♮ (Low two on the "D" string) and then **add** to it a third finger (the note "D") on the "A" string.

Next you move your low two **up** to a **high** two for one note, then it goes back to a low two, but this time on the "A" string.

Now that same second finger changes to "B♭" on the A string and you add the note "G" on the D string at the same time.

Then as you continue to keep that Low one (on the "A" string), your third finger ("G") changes to a Low two (F♮), then slides to a quick, High two, and back to that Low one over three.

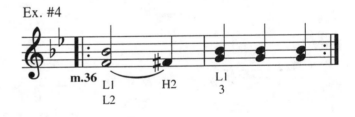

And this changes into a double "A" which we have had a lot of experience with.

Now, lets put all of these parts together! Practice it slowly, and with time you can raise it to the secondary level.

This preparation will help you feel much more comfortable when you get to the double stops. We are ready to learn the notes of MY WILD IRISH ROSE. Here's our first arrangement which will have slides but no other ornaments.

Lesson #50: My Wild Irish Rose
Arrangement #1

Traditional
Arrangement by
Carol Ann Wheeler

Lesson #51: Adding Ornaments to My Wild Irish Rose

Feel free to spend as much time as you want on arrangement #1. When you feel comfortable with those double stops and ready for a new challenge, you can begin adding some decorations.

ORNAMENTS:

Fiddlers each have their own way to decorate tunes. It is part of their style. You will have *your* style, too.

Listen to Lesson #52. Play through arrangement #2 of MY WILD IRISH ROSE. You can decide your own approach: to pick out just a few ornaments and begin adding them one at a time, or maybe you'll choose to add them all at once.

LEARNING TIP:

Don't let decorations interfere with the flow or tempo of the waltz. They should add, not detract, from the beauty of the tune.

If you are having trouble with any decorations, remove them and make them into little mini-exercises, just like I have shown you in this book. Play them over and over. I call this the "broken record" technique. (Know what I mean? Know what I mean? Know what I mean?)

MY WILD IRISH ROSE can be played in lyrical style as we have done here. It can also be played in old-timey style. I have used it in old-time contests and when I do, I put a heavier emphasis on the first beat of each measure, and I play at a bit more brisk tempo.

LILT:

As you listen to Lesson #52 on your learning recording, listen for the *lilt* that I put in. It gives the waltz a feeling of danceability. This lilt is part of my personal style, my trademark.

I did not mark accents over the notes because I was concerned you might overemphasize. Just think of it as *leaning* on the first beat of every measure.

The ornaments I have written in arrangement #2 are some that I enjoy playing. Do not feel that you *have* to play each and every one. That's one of the neat things about fiddling...you have freedom to do things the way you like to *hear* it.

Lesson #52: My Wild Irish Rose
Arrangement #2 - With Ornaments

Traditional
Arrangement by
Carol Ann Wheeler

83

Lesson #53: Woodchoppers' Reel
Arrangement #1

I love every single tune in this book, but surely one of my favorites is WOODCHOPPERS' REEL. I have played it most of my fiddling life. It has served me well in regular contests, old time contests and in Canadian contests. My son Grant heard me play it a lot and, when he was 9 years old, it became one of his tunes.

Since we are already familiar with all of the techniques used in it, let's get started on the bare bones tune.

Here's the basic tune as I hear it.

Traditional
Arranged by
Carol Ann Wheeler

Key of D
Intro = 2 chops & 4 potatoes

Lesson #54: Woodchoppers' Reel

Arrangement #2 – Adding Ornaments

Now we can dress up this tune by adding a few ornaments. Choose as many as you feel you can handle at this time. The tag or shave in our first arrangement could serve if you were trying to create an old-time mood. Here in arrangement #2, I have added one of my favorite Canadian-style endings. If you decide that you like it (I love it!), then use the broken record technique to build your speed on it.

Key of D
Intro = 2 chops & 4 potatoes

Traditional
Arranged by
Carol Ann Wheeler

* I play this ornament sometimes in front of the F♯ note and at other times *after* the F♯ note. Try it both ways.

Lesson #55: Optional FUN ideas for Woodchoppers' Reel

There is nothing wrong with playing only two parts to a tune. For some people, when they have played the same tune for a long time, they may begin to want additional, different ways to play it.

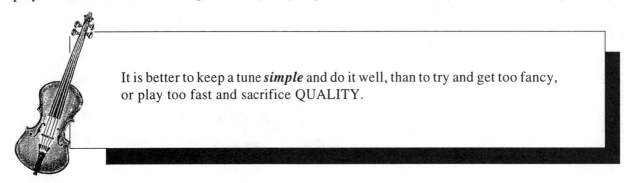

It is better to keep a tune *simple* and do it well, than to try and get too fancy, or play too fast and sacrifice QUALITY.

When you feel ready to add to your WOODCHOPPERS' REEL, here are some ideas I am excited to share with you.

FANCY ENDINGS:

I love to play triplets. They fit beautifully into measure 27 of our Canadian-style ending.

Canadian-style ending without the triplets

Now, just turn those two eighth notes into triplets in measure 27 as shown below:

Canadian-style ending with triplets

Many times a tune has a feature or something about it that helps give it its name. For me I often feel like parts of WOODCHOPPERS' remind me (in my bowing arm) of someone "chopping" wood, especially in this next variation of Part 1. Does it feel that way to you, too? Notice the extra accents? It gives it even more of a choppy feel.

Part 1 – Variation

86

Lesson #56: Part 2 – Optional FUN Variations

Let's turn our attention to Part 2. Here are a couple of techniques that we have already done in this book: the "bow bobble" and the "fat finger" technique.

Variation #1 – Fat Finger Variation

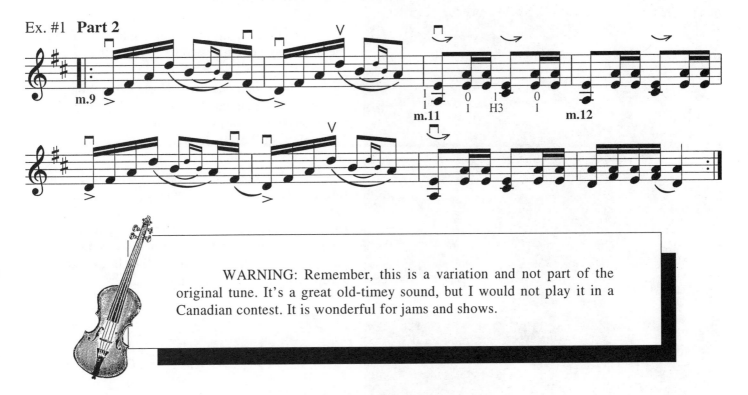

WARNING: Remember, this is a variation and not part of the original tune. It's a great old-timey sound, but I would not play it in a Canadian contest. It is wonderful for jams and shows.

Variation #2 – Scale Down the E

This variation jumps up to the "E" string register.

Variation #3 – Triplet Scale Down the E String

I told you I love triplets. You can take those four eighth-notes that are up high on the "E" string and change them into my old favorite...triplets!

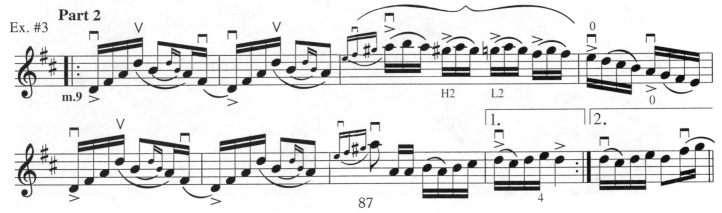

There are special age divisions in today's fiddle contests for young fiddlers. Here you see two fine fiddlers who were Small Fry, Junior Junior, and Junior Fiddle Champions. (Left: Tony Spatz, at age 6, now of Branson, Missouri. Below: Megan Lynch, at age 7, of California.)

Both grew up to be outstanding adult fiddlers, winning countless contests and titles.

Tony went on to win World Champion Junior fiddler. Megan placed 3rd in the Championship Division at the National Fiddle Contest in 1993 (very high) in Weiser, Idaho.

Fiddle contests are very important to some fiddlers. They can motivate you to practice and you can set up goals to strive for. However, you do not have to play in fiddle contests to enjoy your fiddle. There are many ways to have fun – like playing at jams, playing with others in small or large groups, and playing for your own enjoyment.

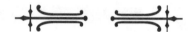

Lesson #57: Building a New Arrangement for Woodchoppers'

Now, let's put it all together in a new, longer, more complicated arrangement as we play along with guitar. If you feel at this time that you need to stick with the original basic Part 2 to get better quality, that's fine. You can add new parts over time as you "grow" into them. You can still play along with John and me on the recording, because all parts blend together. For instance, any of the different Part 2's sound great played together. In fact, Grant and I recorded this tune on our second album, and I might play the "fat finger" part while Grant is coming down that high "E" string part. I think it sounds terrific together. Maybe you have a friend that plays fiddle and you could experiment playing different Part 2's together?

Road Signs

After I have learned a tune and I begin to combine different parts together to form my own arrangement, sometimes I get mixed up in my mind – which part is next, etc. So what I find helps me is to make up little "road signs" along the way. Here, I'll show you what I mean:

First I always like to present the original tune as I learned it. In a small way, I feel I am helping to preserve it. Then if I can, I add some different parts or variations, and I give them little names (road signs) to help me keep them straight in my mind. For instance, in Lesson #56 where I show you three different ways to play Part 2, here are some "road signs": In Variation #1 where I play "fat finger" technique, I don't have time to think all those words, so I just think to myself, "fat!" And in Variation #2, where I have the little scale down the "E" string, I might just have time to think, "scale down!" Then in Variation #3, where I change the little scale into a little triplet scale that goes down, I might think, "trip. down!"

Try using "road signs" and see if you find them helpful. You may come up with your own ideas that work best for you.

And now, here's one of my favorite arrangements of WOODCHOPPERS'. Feel free to add to it, rearrange it, or make up your own arrangement. It's fun to add your own ideas to a tune!

Lesson #57: Woodchoppers' Reel
Arrangement #3

Traditional
Arranged by
Carol Ann Wheeler

Key of D
Intro = 2chops & 4 potatoes

Part 1

Part 2

Part 1 "chopping" variation

Part 2 - "fat finger" variation

Part 1 – original

Part 2 – scale down on E.

Part 2 – repeat – triplets down on E. (optional)

Ending Tag

Lesson #58: East Tennessee Blues

By now you have begun to understand that one tune can have countless arrangements. This is one of the features of fiddling that I love so much. It is fine to play it your own way, to add your personal touch.

This version of EAST TENNESSEE BLUES is one shared with me by my twin fiddle partner, Linda Danielson of Eugene, Oregon. Arrangement #1 is pretty much just as Linda passed it on to me.

LEARNING TIPS:

✔ 1) Remember, you are in the key of "C," so program your "fiddle computer" to be in the finger pattern of "C."

✔ 2) There are some double stops in the second part which can be on the tricky side. If they give you any problems, pull them out and make them into a little practice exercise.

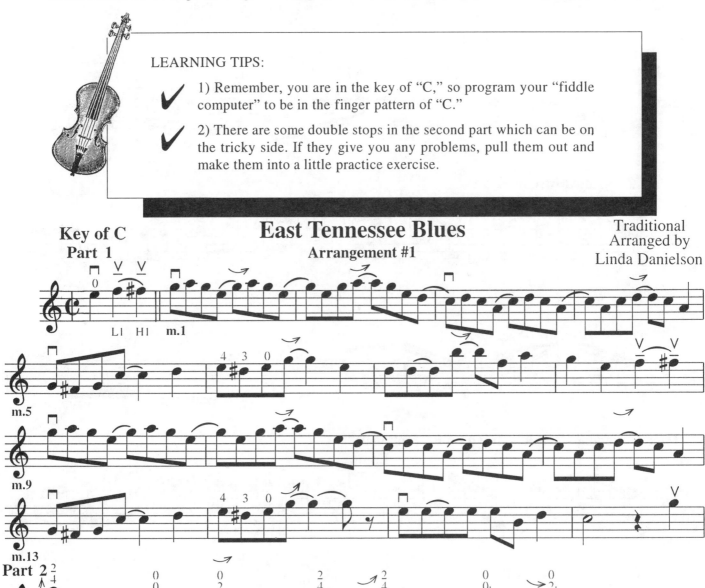

East Tennessee Blues

Arrangement #1

Traditional
Arranged by
Linda Danielson

Key of C
Part 1

Lesson #59: Optional Ideas for East Tennessee Blues

LEARNING TIP:

Just a reminder about the rhythm in EAST TENNESSEE BLUES – it is a "kicky, swingy" rhythm, so what you *see* in the music and what you *hear* on your learning recording are a little different. Listening to, and playing *along* with your recording using earphones will help you *feel* this rhythm.

Here are some ideas that I have added to Linda's arrangement. I like to play Linda's first, then when I repeat, I add some of my ideas. If you choose to play only arrangement #1, you will probably want to at least play Part 1, Part 2, and then return to Part 1 to the end. Playing only arrangement #1 is just fine. When you feel ready for it, or for those of you who want a more complicated arrangement now, you could combine arrangement #1 and #2 together.

Preparing for Arrangement #2 – Other Optional Advanced Licks for East Tennessee Blues

Part 1

Let's first take a look at some of my "fiddlelydiddlies." By understanding *what* I have done to "fiddle" EAST TENNESSEE BLUES, you can eventually use these same ideas to decorate or "fiddle" other tunes that you play.

Measure 2 – I pretty much just change the rhythm. Changing the rhythm in fiddle tunes is a great way to add variety.

Measure 4 – And this same idea (or lick) is used again in measure 4, only this time on the "A" string. Notice that the same fingers and *finger patterns* are used?

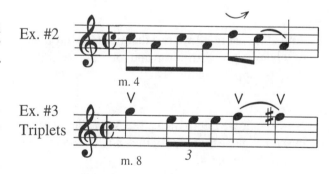

At measure 8, I take the quarter-note "E" and change it into triplets. This just adds a nice little perkiness that the ear hears as something different.

Now this brings us to measure 9 which is just like the beginning again. We could do it exactly the same as in measures 2 and 4, but I will show you a really neat lick that I love. You can decide if you like it enough to give it a try. You have already learned about the "fat finger" technique several times in Volume 1 and 2, but now we use it with pretty rapid finger movements. If you like this sound, it can be yours, too, by simply "paying the price." This is what I am always telling students at workshops. "Paying the price" means that you personally can't *buy* it with money; you must *earn* it by working (practicing).

93

Measures 11 and 12 are the same licks again as measure 9 and 10, only on the middle pair of strings. Same finger patterns, just different strings.

At measures 13 and 14 we can change the rhythm by stretching out the notes into longer "fatter" notes, quarter-note triplets.

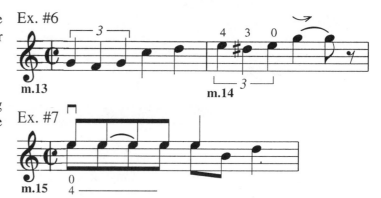

At measure 15 we add a fourth finger "E" along with the open "E" to give a fuller sound (Double E or Drones).

Part 2: Ideas

In measure 19 we use the same notes, but we change our slide. Instead of sliding up into the chord, we play the notes, SLIDE DOWN *out* of the notes, and then slide right back UP.

Notice that this is indicated by a double arrow like this:

At measure 21 we can decorate it, make it a little more fancy by adding a "roll down" (a little scale that moves in a downward direction).

And at measure 23 we use that old familiar idea of changing the rhythm and our old friends, triplets, appear again.

Now when we get to measure 25, we can play it the same or use that idea of the DOUBLE SLIDE like in Example #8.

As we get ready to end our tune, I think that changing the rhythm here, stretching it out into a nice fat TRIPLET, and making it a double "E" really helps give a feeling of "This is the END." If you are not quite ready for the double "E," even the fat "E" string triplet will give you a feeling of finality.

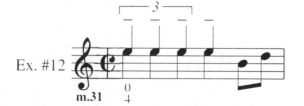

Lesson #60: Putting it all together for a new arrangement

Good for you, sticking with me through these different ideas for EAST TENNESSEE BLUES. Don't feel you have to learn them all in one day. Take one or two a day, or whatever you feel ***you*** can handle. Check them off as you memorize them. And you don't ***have to*** learn them all. You can learn just the ones ***you choose.*** Isn't fiddling fun? You get to make a lot of choices.

So here is arrangement #2 written out with all the new "fiddlelydiddlelies" that we have explored.

East Tennessee Blues

Arrangement #2

Traditional
Arr. Linda Danielson
Carol Ann Wheeler

Key of C
Part 1

Lesson #61: East Tennessee Blues
Arrangement #3

To make it convenient for those of you who wish the challenge of *both* arrangements of EAST TENNESSEE BLUES, here it is all written out for you.

After you have become familiar with it, then try playing along with John and me on your learning recording. In this arrangement we have guitar. Adding guitar is kind of like adding the frosting to a cake for me. It is so much fun to play with guitar, and I think the guitar adds so much to the fiddle sound! If you feel brave (and have stereo equipment), you can turn my fiddle sound down and the guitar up. It will be more like you are playing alone with John.

East Tennessee Blues
Arrangement #3

Part 1 - with variations

Part 2 - with variations

97

Lesson #62: Preparing for There Came an Old Man to My Daddy's Door (Jig)

I love each and every tune in this volume, but surely this next tune is one of my favorite jigs. I learned it about twenty years ago and loved it the first time I heard it. It has served me for jams, shows, and contests. It is a Scottish-Irish jig with four parts, but through the years I have heard that it may be two jigs combined.

If you are new to jig rhythm, it would be good for us to review it. This jig is in 6/8. Much less common are slip jigs which are in 9/8.

Let's practice jig rhythm by playing an open A.

Ex. #1

(Count - 1 2 3 4 5 6 1 2 3 4 5 6)

ABOUT JIG RHYTHM:

When you play jig rhythm, put emphasis on the *first* and *fourth* beats. So while it is in 6/8, you also have a feeling of it being in *two*.

BOWING: When you are using separate bowing in a measure, you will first use a down bow on that first heavy beat and then an up bow on the second heavy beat. For some people this feels awkward, and they feel uncomfortable with their bowing. If it feels different to you, then spend some time practicing exercise #1 at different speeds.

BOWING PATTERNS: I use several patterns of bowing in "OLD MAN" jig. It will help you if you play through all of them and then spend more time practicing any that you find awkward.

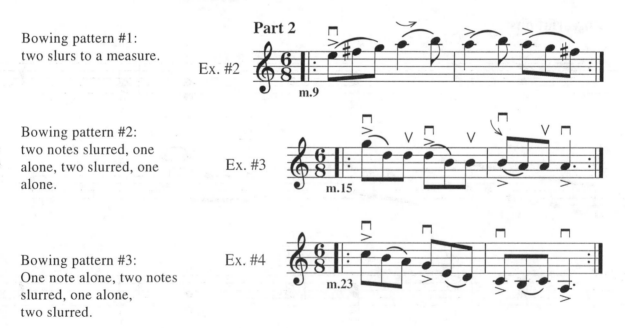

Bowing pattern #1:
two slurs to a measure.

Ex. #2

Bowing pattern #2:
two notes slurred, one alone, two slurred, one alone.

Ex. #3

Bowing pattern #3:
One note alone, two notes slurred, one alone, two slurred.

Ex. #4

This preparation will really help you learn "OLD MAN" quicker. So if you are feeling ready, here's arrangement #1 which will deal with the notes first.

Lesson #63: There Came an Old Man to My Daddy's Door (Jig)

Key of A min
Intro = Two long drags

Traditional
Arrangement by
Carol Ann Wheeler

Lesson #64: Adding Ornaments to "Old Man" Jig

Spend as much time as you wish getting comfortable with the notes in "Old Man" Jig. When you can play along with me (Lesson #63) on your learning recording, begin listening to Lesson #64 of your recording where I play these ornaments. You do not have to add any ornaments, or feel free to add just those that you really like the sound of.

Practicing ornaments alone is a great practice aid. Here are the ornaments I use. Remember they are my style. It is quite possible that other fiddlers would have different ideas for ornaments.

I use a lot of "Roll downs."

Little "roll ups"

At measure 10 there is a fourth finger "flick" (or grace note). For me the fourth finger "flick" feels a bit more clumsy than other fingers. If you find it more tricky, run through this little exercise countless times a day, but never to the point that you overtire your "pinky."

At measure 16, I use a favorite ornament of mine, a one to three "flick."

At measure 25 we have something different, a Cape Breton style of ornament. Instead of flicking notes *above,* you are decorating with notes *below* the note you are decorating. This is not an ornament that you will find in traditional American fiddle music, but I really enjoy adding it to this Scottish-Irish jig.

ORNAMENTS:

It is not necessary for you to tackle all of these ornaments at once. It is fine to work on them and as your fingers get more nimble you can add them to your tunes. You may even come up with some ornament ideas of your own. I think of ornaments as accessories to a tune just like I think of earrings or scarves, etc. as ornaments to a lady's dress (or a tie to a man's suit). They are not absolutely necessary, but they add a little something extra. I might choose certain earrings while someone else might like other earrings. Sometimes the same earrings go with several outfits.

Lesson #64: There Came an Old Man
to My Daddy's Door (Jig)
Arrangement #2

Key of A min
Intro = Two long drags

Traditional
Arranged by
Carol Ann Wheeler

Time to Close

What fun it has been for me to be able to share these tunes with you! I hope you have had as much fun as I. You have come a long way and covered a lot of territory making it through to the end of this volume. Besides enjoyment, I hope you have also absorbed the concept of quality. You could even go back through the book again now, and through reviewing it a second time, pick up more ideas and understanding. Remember, fiddling does take time, so be kind to yourself. Be patient with yourself. If you love the sound of fiddling, DON'T GIVE UP. You *can do it.* Remember that the skills you have learned in Children's Fiddling Method Volumes 1 and 2 can all be added to and used as you explore many of the other fine fiddle books published by Mel Bay.

Sincerest best wishes for continued enjoyment of your music, and see you in Volume 3.

Your fiddle coach,

Carol Ann

Carol Ann